HANDBOOK FOR
MINISTERS OF CARE

Marilyn Kofler, S.P.
Kevin O'Connor

Liturgy Training Publications

Copyright © 1987, Archdiocese of Chicago. Liturgy Training Publications, 1800 North Hermitage Avenue, Chicago IL 60622-1101; 312/486-7008.

Design and Cover Art by Elizandro Carrington.

ISBN 0-930467-59-0

Contents

1. An Introduction to the Ministry of Care........1
2. A Parish Ministry........3
3. Identity: A Person of Prayerful Presence Ministering for a Purpose........5
4. Basic Skills........8
5. Praying Together........14
6. Pastoral Care and the Sacraments........17
7. Pain........26
8. Practical Concerns and Pitfalls........30
9. Your Family and Personal Life........35
10. Evaluating Your Ministry........38
11. Special Problems........40
12. Conclusion........46

Appendix: A Structure for the Ministry of Care........48

CHAPTER 1

AN INTRODUCTION TO THE MINISTRY OF CARE

Perhaps you know some of these people. A very old lady will never leave the nursing home where she has lived these past eight years. A not so very old man is bedridden from an accident that has left him dependent on others for life. Parents keep vigil for their premature newborn. A woman with beautiful, blue eyes is slowly ravaged by disease. A teenager sits alone and afraid in a psychiatric ward. A young child with pneumonia ignores the toys which clutter her room.

They are all ordinary people in extraordinary situations. More than medical attention, they are in need of support and comfort. In a word, they need care. As a minister of care, you visit the sick, the grieving, the aged, the dying. In presence and prayer and sacrament you bring this support and comfort from person to person, uniting the church.

> My brother-in-law died a number of years ago and like many good people we all know, he died after a long bout with cancer. During the six months of his illness a special man came to visit—to talk, to listen, to bring communion, and to represent the local parish. His name was Paul.
>
> Paul was an ordinary man, quiet, steady, but very ordinary, a person like you or me. A discouraged and very sad family came to know Paul well. If there was any doubt that Jesus existed, Paul put our doubts to rest. Jesus was here in this very ordinary man. And when death finally came and went, Paul stayed.

In our gospels we proclaim a Lord who suffers with the suffering, who grieves with the grieving, who knows our isolation, our pain. Every Christian is called to the task of healing and comforting and companionship. But there are those among us with special gifts, gifts that need recognition within our communities. These people can give in the name of the church, in the name of Christ. They can give their gifts in the name of *our* communities, and become the sacramental presence of Christ in our midst.

But ministry is a two-way street. It's never simply "givers" and "receivers," separating the ministers from those to whom they minister. The sick, the grieving, the aged and the dying all have their own gifts to give. For they are signs of Christ suffering and dying in our own flesh and blood. In their troubled minds and bodies the Lord Jesus is alive. Ministers of care will always be given more than they can give, even at times more than they can receive.

As a minister of care you are commissioned by your parish to bring the compassion and communion of the church to the sick and the homebound. But you also have a commission to bear witness to the parish at large: to bring before the whole community the suffering of its members, the suffering of Christ. You become "gift bearers" from parishioner to parishioner, distributing the gifts of the risen Spirit each according to need.

Ministers of care are ordinary people, called to minister to ordinary people in extraordinary circumstances. This book was written to help these ordinary people develop their gifts as they seek to become ministers of care.

CHAPTER 2

A Parish Ministry

"I wonder what it's like to be a minister of care. It must take a special person to be able to deal with so much illness and pain." "Me? I've never prayed with another person out loud." "Nursing homes really frighten me."

"Bringing communion to the elderly is something I've always wanted to do. I really want to visit people in nursing homes, but I'm not sure I'd feel comfortable visiting patients in a hospital." "I just couldn't visit cancer patients—but I'd like to visit others!"

"I'd be good with women and children, but I'm not so sure about visiting men." "I work all day, but I could visit on my lunch hour." "I prefer visiting terminally ill patients. You see, I'm a former nurse and I always regretted the time limitations I had as a professional in dealing with dying patients."

"I've been in and out of hospitals myself and I know how lonely and frightening serious illness can be. A minister of care visited me—and I'd like to be like her." "Prayer has always been important in my life. I'd like to share that with others." "My father died of cancer. I'd like to help others like him." "I'd really like to be a minister of care, but I don't know if I have what it takes."

Each person responds differently to the call to be a minister of care. Every response is colored by experience. Such feelings, fears and hopes need to be aired in a process of discernment, shared reflection with one who is already part of this ministry.

An initial interview with the coordinator/supervisor of a parish's ministry of care deals with the question: "How do I know this is for me?" Ordinarily, the interview will include much listening to the newcomer: his/her hopes and expectations, experiences of illness, the elderly and death. The prospective minister has questions which need answers: How much time will this ministry take? How will I know what to do? How do I know I can do a good job? The coordinator will discuss the specific goals of the ministry of care, the training and ongoing enrichment involved, the expected time commitment. The interview itself is the opportunity for both the prospective minister and the coordinator to discern a commitment to the training program and involvement in this ministry.

Most training programs include at least six two-hour sessions which focus on ministry, basic skills for pastoral visitation, the experience of illness, the aging process, death and dying, prayer and pastoral visitation, and eucharistic ministry to the sick. At the conclusion of the training program the new ministers of care are commissioned, usually at a Sunday Mass in the parish.

Ongoing formation and supervision are most important to nourish and sustain the ministers of care. A two-hour session held once a month provides for continuing formation, offers an opportunity for reflection on experiences, becomes a forum to discuss questions and problems, and is the occasion for peer support, shared prayer and growth in ministry. Business is kept to a minimum at these sessions.

Once a year it is important to gather and look at the original goals, expectations and commitments, and to evaluate them in light of the experiences of the individual ministers of care.

Is this a lifetime commitment? No. Closure is a very important element for such a commitment. Ministers of care (as well as other ministers) need to know they have completed a commitment successfully. They need to know that it is acceptable and even expected that they will "retire" or go on to a different form of involvement. The expected commitment as a minister of care can be for one, two or three years. When the period of commitment comes to a close, it is important that the minister and supervisor take time together to discern whether to renew the commitment.

CHAPTER 3

IDENTITY:
A PERSON OF PRAYERFUL PRESENCE MINISTERING FOR A PURPOSE

The Person

Ministry of care is one of the oldest ministries in the church. It was a ministry open to all the baptized that gradually, through the ages, became a ministry for priests and religious, especially those who established and served in hospitals. The renewal of this ministry among all who are baptized is one of the many good works to come from Vatican II. Ministry of care thrives today as people within the community minister to one another's needs.

It has become clear to many in parish work that the pastoral care of the sick, the elderly, and the dying requires not only serious commitment from the parish, but the presence of carefully trained volunteers with professional direction.

When a parishioner needs this type of pastoral care, the coordinator contacts a minister of care to make a pastoral visit.

This ministry is a powerful witness to God's presence. It is a service to others that is humbling and at times frustrating, but it is a significant means of sharing in Christ's healing power. This ministry is both a sign of hope and an intimate sharing of the good news.

The Prayer

As a minister of care you know from experience about two forms of praying.

Prayers from tradition are one form. The "Our Father" is such a ritual prayer. So are the psalms and many hymns and songs. These prayers allow you to join your voice to the whole church. When you repeat them again and again, perhaps when you even memorize them, they become alive in you. They are one way you give to your life the very shape of the gospel. They say something important about how you feel, and about what you want to be.

There is also a kind of prayer that allows you to hear. This is the prayer of listening. It is listening to the spirit, recognizing God's movement and words in your life.

Ritual prayer and prayer-as-listening are both life-giving activities. They are responses in faith to your position in the world, to your belief about yourself, and to your belief about God.

Frequently, in your ministry, you may find yourself centering on prayer of petition. With some conscious effort to find other dimensions in prayer, you can praise, bless and thank God and express also the sorrow and desire for forgiveness that is deep in Christian life.

Ministers of care gradually learn how broad and many-sided, yet how simple, prayer is. They become at home with prayer as thanksgiving, prayer as petition, prayer as praise, prayer as sorrow.

The Presence

Your presence is who you are more than what you say or do. You know this from experience. You can look back at certain people who have entered your life and lifted you: perhaps a family member or someone you knew only briefly. Ministers of care are people who provide that kind of presence.

We cannot make any once-and-for-all list of what it takes to have such a presence to others. Perhaps you can think of persons who were encouraging to you, persons who gave you hope, persons who allowed you to see how you needed to come to grips with yourself, people who saw something that was inside you and brought it forth.

The Purpose

First, you are a representative from your faith community. You are to be yourself, but to be from others. You come to a particular person in faith to witness that the faith is alive in your local community, that these Christians truly do love one another.

Second, you are to engage this person in a relationship. You are seeking something like the kind of saving relationship that helped others come to know Jesus through faith. In his relationships, Jesus did four things for people. He gave them life, he encouraged them, he showed great trust for them, and he released them to themselves. Those whom

Jesus touched never became dependent on him. Through a saving kind of relationship with them, he released them.

That is the real key to ministry of care. You need to create a relationship as Jesus did. You need to give life and to encourage and develop the kind of relationship that allows people to trust themselves, to trust you, to trust the Lord.

Third, you are a prayerful example of God's presence. You are there in front of a person in great need saying, "God wants you to come close." You are also a witness of your own personal faith: This is what God's presence in my life means to me.

CHAPTER 4

BASIC SKILLS

Ministers of care are first and foremost helpers. They respond to this ministry because they see the need and feel the desire to help. But the kind of help varies with the people and the situation.

In the ministry of care, the *way* the minister responds is the help itself.

Everyone has had friends who, with the best intentions, have tried to comfort them in a time of need. At wakes and funerals, in hospital waiting rooms and at home, people have said the wrong thing. Everyone has done it.

This chapter is about what to do, how to do it, what to say, how to say it. As helpers, you need to be more than friends. You must become capable of ministering effectively to people you have not known previously.

A PASTORAL VISIT

Given this caution, it can be helpful to distinguish between a pastoral and a social visit. Friends make social visits—and that is fine. Ministers make pastoral visits—and that requires something different.

A social visit concentrates on:

- Talking about the weather, people and events
- Maintaining a friendly atmosphere
- Sharing mutual stories

- Entertaining
- Comforting, sometimes by avoiding painful topics

In contrast, a pastoral visit concentrates on:

- The person's thoughts, feelings, reflections and experiences
- Accepting problems as they now exist
- Helping the person share himself or herself
- Comforting through facing and sharing the pain
- The person's relationship with God

How do you get yourself ready to give this kind of help? One quality you will need might be called *quiet patience.*

If you consider that the people you will visit are surrounded by concerns—physical pain, the welfare of family, anxiety over the future—it may be easier to see the need for such quiet patience.

Patience is defined as "forebearance or painstaking care towards others." The focus is *on the other* and this otherness is the premier quality for the minister of care.

Your own quiet is a manifestation of such patience. It permits a wider range of responses from the people you visit. Often full of self-concern, the sick person needs someone to listen. To listen effectively, the minister of care needs to be quiet.

Everyone loves to talk. It sets you at ease, allows you to make connections, and permits you to *do* something. But ministers of care are called upon to encourage the *other* person to talk. This is not easy . . . for anyone.

Good Listening

How do you listen with quiet patience? Here are three helps.

- *Attend.* Physically pay attention. Use your eyes to look into the person's eyes. Position your body straight on so she or he can see you. Look interested.
- *Notify.* Let the person know that you have heard what has been said. Nod occasionally. Lean forward to express your interest.
- *Develop (and dig).* Ask questions. As you hear something of interest, ask more specific questions. Allow time for reflection.

"Notify" and "develop" are often difficult skills to acquire. They have much to do with your response to what you hear. The five Rs of effective listening are listed in order of difficulty with the easiest listed first.

Repeat Say precisely what you heard the person say. Repeat it back. This will feel "funny," but only to you. It won't feel funny to the person to whom you are speaking. Use the *exact words* the person used.

Restate Here again, repeat what was said, but use *your own words*. This will feel more comfortable for you, but it is possible that your meaning won't match the person's meaning. If you find that your interpretation is not quite right, then go back and repeat word for word, phrase by phrase.

Reflect In addition to repeating or restating, the skill of reflecting allows you to *act as a mirror for the feelings* of the person. Underneath much of what is said are the person's deeper feelings. The tone of what is said will reveal those feelings. Here the listener attempts gently to identify the feelings heard (sad, angry, happy, scared, hurt).

Respond Sometimes words are not enough. *Tears* and *laughter* express what words can't. *Touch* helps us communicate across the words. *Silence* allows for a deeper sense of understanding. A *nod* gives support. These responses signal your attentive listening and go beyond words.

Respect Whenever you listen, this last skill needs to permeate your relationship with the person.

A Possible Routine

What is to be changed, improved, is not yourself but your talent for this particular kind of ministry. This is similar to changing the way you talk to a boss, a coworker, a spouse. You change the *way* you talk, not yourself. You learn to adjust to the person and the circumstances. The same is true with this ministry.

The preparation that goes into a visit can greatly influence your listening. Here is an example of a helpful regimen before a hospital visit. These five steps can be used on each occasion.

- *The ride over.* This is your opportunity to "settle yourself." Turn off the radio and reflect. Pray over your ministry. Sort out your day and let it take a back seat to your visit.
- *The chapel visit.* Find the hospital chapel (or surgery waiting room) for some structured quiet time for yourself.

- *The nurses' station.* Check with the nurses. Tell them who you are, why you are there and ask if it is proper to visit at this time. Sometimes the nurses will advise you of recent medication, pain or sleep patterns.
- *The visit itself.* Knock on the door even if it is open, announce yourself clearly and loudly, ask permission to come in. Do these things for every visit. This routine shows the same respect that you would give if visiting a person's home: the hospital room is someone's home for a time.
- *The follow-up.* After each visit, ask yourself: "What needs to be done?" "How do I feel about this visit?" Take care of the task and take care of yourself. If necessary, see your parish coordinator for help and your group for support.

GUIDELINES FOR A VISIT

Ministers of care frequently request guidelines. Many have found the following to be useful.

- *Be friendly.* Be as you are when you want to be seen as friendly. Be cheerful, open and warm.
- *Be flexible.* Every visit is different. Be prepared for nothing to be routine. Interruptions may happen. You will be a better visitor if you can "go with the flow."
- *Be alert.* Be aware of the events, the people, the environment.
- *Be confident.* No one is an expert all the time. Even the best ministers of care are not always as confident as they would like to be. But an air of confidence will help tremendously. Even if you don't feel confident, quietly act as though you do. It will help you and the person you visit.
- *Be personal.* Feel free to ask questions, speak of feelings, listen intently, nod, and respect what is being told to you. That doesn't mean that every visit delves into deep or intimate matters. Another sort of flexibility is called for here. It is the other's needs that are primary, not your own, and some will want and need nothing more than a rather pleasant visit.
- *Be yourself.* You'll be at your best when you can be uniquely you within the context of your ministerial role (a person of prayerful presence).

Using Your Emotions

Psychologist Eugene Kennedy has written extensively on how to be a listening helper. One aspect of this is listening to your own emotions. Knowing yourself and your emotions is a critical skill for the listening helper. Awareness of the following questions before and after each ministry of care visit can be helpful.

Before the visit:
    How do I feel today?
    How do I feel about going on this visit today?
    Do I have any strong feelings about something else that might preoccupy me?

After the visit:
    How do I feel now?
    What feelings have stayed with me?
    Which feelings do I need to reflect on?
    Which feelings do I need to talk about with someone else?

Emotions and feelings are not alien beings. They give valuable information about yourself if only you recognize them and accept them.

Ministers of care may discover some emotions they do not otherwise experience. You are called on continually to exercise good judgment regarding these. Ask yourself: Should I ignore how I feel? How do I get rid of the feeling that I have right now?

There are certainly no absolute rules regarding these emotions, but some guidelines may help. Psychiatrist Karen Horney has identified three ways that people move in relationship to one another: toward, away and against. Review your past day and consider the times you have moved:

Toward the times you reached out, enjoyed, and enabled
Away the times you ignored, omitted or excluded
Against the angry times, the quarrels, the complaining

Applying these to ministry of care, you will find that certain feelings will move you in one or more of these three directions with the person or the family you are visiting:

Toward the "warm" emotions: happy, glad, enjoyable
Away the "cooler" emotions: afraid, disgusted, disappointed
Against the "hot" emotions: angry, jealous, hateful

Depending on your experience and your interpretation of that experience, you respond in your unique way to the different people that you visit and to the many things that are happening to them. When you sense some strong emotion, try to recall times when you had a similar experience. Your own past may help you gain an understanding of your present emotions.

It is less important to get rid of emotions that are troublesome to you than it is to recognize them. The next time that you are filled with an emotion that is giving you difficulty, don't simply force your way past it. Try to recognize it. Put a name on it, try to determine where it came from, and then accept it. This will take you a long way in knowing about yourself and the person you are visiting.

CHAPTER 5

PRAYING TOGETHER

As a minister of care you are a representative of your parish. As such, you unite the prayer of the community with the prayer of the people you visit. This prayer raises a number of practical questions: What style of prayer is best? What if you are unable to pray, or the people you visit do not want to pray? How can you balance praise and thanksgiving with petitionary prayer? Which are better, formal prayers or informal, spontaneous prayers?

Leading spontaneous prayers is an art which needs developing. It is grounded in the art of listening and a genuine sensitivity to the person to whom you minister. In the beginning of your ministry, perhaps it is wisest to limit yourself to formal prayers. Eventually, you may want to combine both forms of prayer. Whether formal or informal, the pattern of Christian prayer is the Lord's Prayer. We address God intimately and lovingly, and then we bless God. God's reign is welcomed. God's will is accepted. Only after we offer our thanks and praise do we make our petitions in confidence, and ask forgiveness in humility.

Here is a list of prayers that you should know well: the Lord's Prayer, the Hail Mary, the Glory Be, Psalm 23 ("The Lord is my shepherd"), Psalm 121 ("I lift up my eyes to the mountains"), Psalm 130 ("Out of the depths"), the Magnificat, the Confiteor, the eucharistic acclamations ("Dying you destroyed our death . . .").

Good sources of prayers in visiting the sick, elderly, and homebound include *Pastoral Care of the Sick: Rite of Anointing and Viaticum* (the church's official rite available in editions published by Catholic Book Publishing Company and the Liturgical Press); *Teach Me to Pray* by Gabe Huck (William H. Sadlier, Inc.); and *Day by Day: The Notre*

Dame Prayerbook for Students, edited by Thomas McNally and William G. Storey (Ave Maria Press). Confer with the coordinator of the ministry of care if you plan to use written prayers that are less familiar: many published prayers are not rich in the lived tradition of the church.

In your ministry of care you may be unable to pray. Everyone has times when they are unable to put words to their prayer, when they are uncomfortable, dry, frustrated or distracted. There are times when your presence will have to suffice as an act of prayer, especially during visits when matters get beyond your control. There may be little you can do in such circumstances. But it does help to focus on the purpose of your visit beforehand: perhaps you are there to be a silent witness to the presence of the church. Perhaps you are there to pray for someone rather than with someone.

We already discussed ways to focus your purpose by giving yourself some silence and time for reflection before you visit in order to open yourself to God's Spirit. When you become comfortable in the art of praying aloud with others, ask the people you visit if they would like to pray. Ask directly, being sensitive to the present moment and the person you are visiting.

If they say no, realize that, like yourself, there are times when others cannot pray or even listen to the prayer of others. It may be a simple matter of embarrassment. Or it may be as complicated as someone being unable to accept the will of God, and unable to see any reason for giving thanks. It's difficult to second guess what others may be thankful for or what others hope for. But you may be able to give thanks for the person you are visiting, for their families, for the community you represent. And you are always able to give thanks to God for the Lord Jesus.

Our prayer with people in trouble may tend towards petitionary prayer, for health or strength or freedom. But Christian prayer is of its essence *eucharistic*, prayer of praise and thanksgiving, prayer of self-offering, and this is precisely the form of communal prayer most often denied the homebound, the hospitalized and the imprisoned. It may be well and good to pray for healing, comfort, release from anxiety and acceptance of present situations. But in the end, as a representative of a eucharistic community, you are there standing before another human being to give God praise and glory.

Develop your ability to pray spontaneously. Instead of putting words into other people's mouths, review the "five Rs of effective listening" on page 10. Reflect on the situation at hand and the concerns of the people you visit. Think of ways to address God as the source of life, comfort, healing and joy. Following the pattern of the Lord's Prayer, address God intimately. Pour out your blessings to God. Ask for blessings, not only for the person you are visiting, but for their family, parish, city. Pray for the church and the world. Gather up your prayer with words of glory, such as the prayer "Glory to the Father..."

Never forget that the people you visit can make their praise a gift to the community of the church. As a minister of care you risk thinking of prayer as a one-way street, something you can do for them. Yet the church understands the sacrament of the sick to be a celebration of what the sick do for us: they glorify God in their own flesh and blood, in their suffering and in their recovery. We lose too much when we forget what the people we visit can do for us and for the community of the church. Enable the people you visit to pray for you, to pray for each other, to make their prayer a gift to the church. Let them know that the cross they bear and the joys they witness are in themselves acts of praise to God.

CHAPTER 6

PASTORAL CARE AND THE SACRAMENTS

Ministers of care need a good understanding of the rites for anointing the sick, communion of the sick, reconciliation, and pastoral care of the dying. For English speaking and Spanish-speaking communities, these rites have been collected in a book: *Pastoral Care of the Sick: Rites of Anointing and Viaticum* (available from Catholic Book Publishing Company or The Liturgical Press).

The Spanish translation of this text, *Cuidado Pastoral de los Enfermos* is published by Buena Prensa (Mexico City). A bilingual, abridged edition is available from Liturgy Training Publications. All of the rites discussed below are found in *Pastoral Care of the Sick.* The following is an outline of the book's contents.

Part I: PASTORAL CARE OF THE SICK
   Introduction
   Chapter One: Visits to the Sick
   Chapter Two: Visits to a Sick Child
   Chapter Three: Communion of the Sick
      Communion in Ordinary Circumstances
      Communion in a Hospital or Institution
   Chapter Four: Anointing of the Sick
      Anointing outside Mass
      Anointing within Mass
      Anointing in a Hospital or Institution

Part II: PASTORAL CARE OF THE DYING
   Introduction

Chapter Five: Celebration of Viaticum
 Viaticum within Mass
 Viaticum outside Mass

Chapter Six: Commendation of the Dying

Chapter Seven: Prayers for the Dead

Chapter Eight: Rites for Exceptional Circumstances
 Continuous Rite of Penance, Anointing, and Viaticum
 Rite for Emergencies
 Christian Initiation for the Dying

Part III: READINGS, RESPONSES, AND VERSES FROM SACRED SCRIPTURE
 Appendix
 Rite for Reconciliation of Individual Penitents

Some may feel hesitation in approaching *Pastoral Care of the Sick*. After all, it is a book of rituals, and most of us still seem to feel that this is the business of the ordained. But this book is too important to be left to the ordained. The introductions it offers to the whole area of pastoral care, and specifically to visiting the sick, to anointing and to viaticum, should be required reading for all ministers of care. Required—but helpful and enjoyable, and capable of stimulating much discussion and sharing.

As a minister of care, you need to become so familiar with this book that you are truly at home within it: knowing where to find the rites for visiting the sick, for communion, for viaticum, for praying with the dying and with the family after a death. You need also to explore the various "options" that are provided: a rich resource of scripture readings and prayers found in the final sections of the book. Knowing these well, you can find the most appropriate reading or prayer even when there is little time for preparation.

Careful reading of *Pastoral Care of the Sick* will also teach the minister about being the leader of these rituals. That is not so threatening as it may sound, but it does imply a great responsibility. There is an art to leading prayer: to the words and gestures, to the silences. This is, in fact, the most *personal* prayer the church possesses, but it becomes so only when people make it their own. As a minister of care, you need to have a sense for these rites, a familiarity with what is primary and what is secondary so that the ritual may do its work of forming and strengthening the church.

VISITS TO THE SICK

The rite outlined in *Pastoral Care of the Sick* follows the common pattern of reading, response, prayer and blessing. This is a good preparation for a future visit during which the sick person will receive communion. The rite includes readings which speak of the mystery of human suffering in the words, works and life of Christ. The readings of the day or of the Sunday (just past or coming) found in the lectionary may also be used and are a means of helping the sick person feel connected with the worship of the church. The Sunday scripture readings (usually just one of them at a single visit) are especially important. They are a way of uniting the sick person with the gathered church. These readings may be found in *At Home with the Word* (Liturgy Training Publications) or in a Sunday missal. When using a missal, you will need to know the name of the Sunday and which "cycle" (the scriptures follow a three-year cycle) is being read by the church this year. Prayers drawn from the psalms or from litanies or other prayers may follow the reading.

Visits to a Sick Child

The minister begins by establishing a friendly and easy relationship with the child. It is important that the minister help the child understand that the sick are very special in the eyes of God. The rite consists of a brief reading from scripture, simple prayers taken from scripture which can be repeated by the child, familiar prayers (such as the Lord's Prayer, the Hail Mary, litanies, or a simple form of general intercessions) and a blessing.

Communion of the Sick

In preparing the prayers and readings for the rite of communion of the sick, keep in mind the condition of the sick person. The readings and any "brief explanation" should lead those present to a deeper understanding of the mystery of human suffering in relation to the dying and rising of Jesus Christ. Bringing communion to the sick is a powerful symbol of the unity between the local faith community and its sick members. In ordinary circumstances the rite of communion includes:

INTRODUCTORY RITES
    Sprinkling with Holy Water
    Penitential Rite

LITURGY OF THE WORD
  Reading
  Response
  General Intercessions
LITURGY OF HOLY COMMUNION
  The Lord's Prayer
  Communion
  Silent Prayer
  Prayer after Communion
CONCLUDING RITE
  Blessing

Remembering the general principle that sacraments happen only in the context of relationship, *the rite of communion preferably follows an initial visit during which some relationship is established between the minister and sick person.*

In celebrating the rite of communion in a hospital or institution, care must be taken so that this rite is not diminished to the absolute minimum. When it is not possible to celebrate the full rite, the following may be substituted:

INTRODUCTORY RITE
  Antiphon
LITURGY OF HOLY COMMUNION
  Greeting
  The Lord's Prayer
  Communion
CONCLUDING RITE
  Concluding Prayer

The rite may begin with the recitation of the antiphon in the church, the hospital chapel, or the first room visited. The concluding prayer may be said in the church, the hospital chapel, or the last room visited. No blessing is given. In each room, with each patient, the minister greets the patient and leads the Lord's Prayer before communion.

ANOINTING OF THE SICK

By the sacred anointing of the sick and the prayer of its presbyters, the whole church commends the sick to the suffering and glorified Lord so that he may raise them up and save them (see James 5:14-16). The church exhorts them, moreover, to contribute to the welfare of the people of God by associating themselves willingly with the passion and death of Christ (see Romans 8:17; Colossians 1:24; 2 Timothy 2:11-12; Peter 4:13).

Vatican II: *Constitution on the Church*, #11

The sacrament of the anointing of the sick is given to those who are seriously ill by anointing them on the forehead and hands with blessed olive oil or, according to circumstances, with another blessed plant oil and saying once only these words:

> Through this holy anointing
> may the Lord in his love and mercy help you
> with the grace of the Holy Spirit.
>
> May the Lord who frees you from sin
> save you and raise you up.

Apostolic Constitution on the
Sacrament of the Anointing of the Sick

The celebration of this sacrament of anointing consists in the laying on of hands by the priests of the church, the offering of the prayer of faith, and the anointing with oil made holy by God's blessing.

Through the sacrament of anointing the church supports the sick in their struggle against illness and continues the healing ministry of Jesus Christ. This sacrament is not to be delayed but is best celebrated at times when the sick person is capable of active participation. Celebrating this sacrament with family members and other members of the Christian community enhances the fullness of the significance of the church's prayer and encounter with the Lord.

Prayers, suggestions for readings, and blessings are found in *Pastoral Care of the Sick*.

The minister of care shows great concern in providing for the anointing of the person whose health is seriously impaired by sickness or old age. Again, this is done in accord with the person's wishes.

The celebration of this sacrament is not to be delayed until death or the danger of death is imminent.

The sacrament may be repeated if the person recovers after being anointed and becomes ill once more. The sacrament may also be repeated if during the same illness the person's condition becomes more serious.

Elderly persons may be anointed if they have become notably weakened even though their life is not threatened by serious illness.

Anointing outside Mass

When the anointing of those whose health is seriously impaired by sickness or old age occurs outside Mass, the rite is as follows:

INTRODUCTORY RITES
    Greeting
    Sprinkling with Holy Water
    Instruction
    Penitential Rite

LITURGY OF THE WORD
    Reading
    Response

LITURGY OF ANOINTING
    Litany
    Laying on of Hands
    Prayer over the Oil
    Anointing
    Prayer after Anointing
    The Lord's Prayer

(LITURGY OF HOLY COMMUNION)
    Communion
    Silent Prayer
    Prayer after Communion

CONCLUDING RITE
    Blessing

Anointing within Mass

The sacrament of anointing, when celebrated within Mass, is as follows:

INTRODUCTORY RITES
    Greeting
    Reception of the Sick
    Penitential Rite
    Opening Prayer

LITURGY OF THE WORD

LITURGY OF ANOINTING
    Litany
    Laying on of Hands
    Prayer over the Oil

Anointing
Prayer after Anointing

LITURGY OF THE EUCHARIST

CONCLUDING RITES
Blessing
Dismissal

PASTORAL CARE OF THE DYING

The ministry to the dying places emphasis on trust in the Lord's promise of life that never ends rather than on the struggle against illness. *Pastoral Care of the Sick* contains a collection of prayers which support and comfort the Christian who is dying. These prayers are traditionally called the commendation of the dying. Also included are prayers for the dead, as well as rites to be used in cases of emergency.

In the Introduction to "Celebration of Viaticum" (Chapter Five in *Pastoral Care of the Sick*) it is pointed out that if the sacrament of anointing of the sick is celebrated at the beginning of a serious illness then viaticum, celebrated when death is close, will be better understood as the last sacrament of Christian life.

It is important that the minister of care understand that sacraments are celebrated for the living, not for the dead. In the case of death, the minister of care may lead the surviving family members in prayers for the dead and may conclude these prayers with a simple blessing or with a symbolic gesture, e.g., the sign of the cross, that speaks of Christian life that is changed, not taken away. In addition to the prayer found in *Pastoral Care of the Sick* (#221 and #222, "Prayer after Death"), the minister should be familiar with #104–108 in the *Order of Christian Funerals*; this is a section of prayers to be used with the family soon after death has occurred.

Viaticum

Viaticum is the final reception of communion when there is danger of death from any cause. During the celebration of viaticum, it is desirable for Christians to renew the faith professed at baptism.

The ordinary ministers of viaticum are parish priests and chaplains. Ministers of communion to the sick may administer viaticum in cases of necessity or with the permission of the pastor.

The General Introduction to *Pastoral Care of the Sick* provides information to guide the minister of care in discerning the readiness of a person for the anointing of the sick or the sacrament of viaticum. The minister should become familiar with the rite for "Viaticum outside Mass." The outline is as follows:

INTRODUCTORY RITES
    Greeting
    Sprinkling with Holy Water
    Instruction
    Penitential Rite
    [Apostolic Pardon]
LITURGY OF THE WORD
    Reading
    Homily
    Baptismal Profession of Faith
    Litany
LITURGY OF VIATICUM
    The Lord's Prayer
    Communion as Viaticum
    Silent Prayer
    Prayer after Communion
CONCLUDING RITES
    Blessing
    Sign of Peace

The introductory comments on viaticum in *Pastoral Care of the Sick* state the following:

> This rite includes some of the elements of the Mass, especially a brief liturgy of the word. Depending on the circumstances and the condition of the dying person, this rite should also be a communal celebration. Every effort should be made to involve the dying person, family, friends, and members of the local community in the planning and celebration. The manner of celebration and the elements of the rite which are used should be accommodated to those present and the nearness of death. (#186)

> An abbreviated liturgy of the word, ordinarily consisting of a single biblical reading, gives the minister an opportunity to explain the word of God in relation to viaticum. The sacrament should be described as sacred food which strengthens the Christian for the passage through death to life in sure hope of the resurrection. (#188)

SENSITIVITY

Sensitivity to the patient is crucial. "Is there anything the church can do for you?" is a question that gives freedom to the nonpracticing Catholic as well as to the one who regularly participates in the sacramental life of the church. The responses can vary. "No, thanks, your visit is sufficient." "I'd like to see a priest." "I'd really like to receive communion." The skilled minister of care responds appropriately to the specific request either with closure or with a promise to contact a priest or with the offer to bring communion—and then follows through.

An understanding of the rites for anointing the sick, communion to the sick, and reconciliation, as well as some basic principles of pastoral care, are extremely important for ministers of care. The initial training program provides insight and opportunity for dialogue about these. Continuing education programs and reflection sessions support and deepen the underlying theology contained in these rites.

CHAPTER 7

PAIN

Some of you will be visiting people in hospitals. Hospitals can be very painful places, not just physically, but also spiritually, mentally, emotionally. Though many hospitals attempt to treat the patient as a complete person, it is primarily the body that they are responsible for, and sometimes bodies have to have needles put into them, electrodes attached, tests done.

Those entering the hospital have their closest possessions taken away—their clothes. They are left with the hospital's gown. They are usually surrounded by strangers who are in various stages of illness. Almost everyone who enters a hospital is afraid. They are afraid of what is happening and what might happen. They are filled with memories of what has happened to family and friends, and perhaps even to themselves.

A minister of care who visits those in the hospital needs to hold certain convictions about pain:

- *Pain is real.* When a person is in pain, there is no denying his or her discomfort. No matter what you hear, no matter what you believe, always work as if the person's pain is real.
- *Pain is personal.* A person's pain and the response to that pain are deeply personal. The pain is contained within the person's own physical body and the response lives in his or her own psychological self.
- *Pain is a subjective experience.* Only the patient can best define what she or he is feeling. Respect the patient's own description. And don't talk about your own pain.

- *Pain can reassure.* Strange as it may seem, for some people pain reassures them that what they expected is indeed happening according to schedule. This belief may lessen the pain for some.
- *Pain can provoke fear.* Many people fear the phone call to the dentist. What must surgery, cancer or blindness provoke even in the most courageous?
- *Pain can be momentary or go on as if without end.* Bursts of pain can shock the senses and send a person reeling. Unrestricted and seemingly unending pain can test endurance. This is often a time of intense concentration and loneliness.
- *The fear of pain is not always related to the pain itself.* Anticipated pain can be a real terror. The mix of the physical and the psychological can be hard to communicate, and hard for a visitor to appreciate.
- *Disease causes dis-ease.* All ill health is stressful.

Those who visit the sick and who come away with true compassion are those who really attempt to understand what it's like for that particular person. A wise supervisor of counselors once said, "You won't know what this person is really like until you know what their life is like *for them.*"

What is pain like for you as a human being, and not just as a minister of care? From a stomach ache to a toothache, from a bad back to something that requires hospitalization—you know something of this. And you know pain that is spiritual and emotional. You know what pain is like for you, and you know how difficult it is to communicate this to another person. Frequently, what you need most are people to be there with you, to nod their heads and to say, "We're here for you." You *don't* need to hear:

"Don't worry, everything will work out."

"I had that operation once too."

"I've had a really bad day!"

"My doctor disagrees."

"I know what you are going through."

"It can't be that bad, can it?"

Suffering is made more tolerable through friendship, through caring. Those who have been there can be your teachers. The reflection which follows was written by Caroline Arnold and Patricia Ismert.

Inside my body is a person—ME! Please listen to me, feel with me and for me. Even though I am sometimes helpless, treat me as an adult. Don't make me submit like a child to bewildering routines. Please preserve my now fragile dignity. Enable me to keep my self respect. Don't strip me of my identity when you strip me of my clothes. Don't make me beg for relief of pain. Don't act as if I'm unintelligent because I do not know about my body. Don't treat my body like a machine in a repair shop.

I beg you to remember that illness, pain and fear bring on overly emotional and sometimes seemingly unreasonable behavior. These unknown surroundings bewilder me. When you remain a stranger to me, my fears cause me to behave in a manner even more unreasonable. Look at me when you speak to me, even briefly, just so I know I am not forgotten.

Make the things you must do to me more bearable. Call me by name. Tell me who you are. Touch me. Tell me what you are going to do—even though you've told me before. The sound of your voice, the feel of your touch reminds me that I am not alone. Show me your compassion. Let me see it in your face. Let me hear it in your voice. Let me know by your gentle, caring touch. Show me, through your care, that I am a person.

Don't take away my privacy when you intrude in your helpful way to care for me. Everything is so open here and I am a very private person. Knock on my door before you enter my room. Pull the curtains around my bed. Cover me when you bathe me. Keep my door closed if I request it.

I bring not only my sick body to you, I bring with me my total being. I am a suffering human being. Think not only of my body but also of my spirit. Offer me spiritual care. Pray with me or for me. Cry with me if you feel the need. You may be my closest friend at that moment. You will make my life bearable until my family or someone important to me arrives. I am weak, fragile and vulnerable. Help me to be strong.

Respect me, even though my body is wrinkled with age or made unsightly by disease. Don't abandon me and leave me like a helpless prisoner. Don't isolate me with your rituals. When I feel your discomfort, my day becomes bleak.

Outside my door the disembodied voices call to each other. Your laughter and joy make me long to be included. How I need someone to laugh with, to share joy with. The constant paging: who are those people? Carts clatter by my door. Between these are the seemingly never-ending klinking, clatter, bumps and rattles that no one explains.

Give me care so that I will not be so fearful. Then I know that you will make the suffering bearable and keep hope alive so that some joy may enter my life again. Knowing this will make my days brighter and my nights shorter.

CHAPTER 8

PRACTICAL CONCERNS AND PITFALLS

OPENING AND CLOSING

In making the hospital visit, introduce yourself clearly and distinctly. "My name is Pat Smith. I am a minister of care from St. Mary's. The pastor asked me to stop in to see how you are doing." This tells the person who you are, where you are from, and indicates someone the sick person might know on the parish staff. Your opening line does not have to be well rehearsed, but it needs to be genuine. Next, you might relate to the situation: "How are you doing?" "How are things going here?" "How can I help you?" These are all appropriate questions that may lead to a conversation. This is where you use all your skills for listening and understanding, for sharing yourself and representing your community.

The visit may come to a close because of your schedule, because visiting hours are almost over, because the doctor or other visitors arrive. It is appropriate, but optional, to talk about another visit. If you can make another visit, say something like, "Would it be okay if I stopped back tomorrow?" You may also ask, "Will it be okay if another minister of care visits you?" Do not talk about coming back unless you are absolutely certain you can. Then it is time to say goodbye and to go. It also is a time to think to yourself, "What should I do as a result of this visit?"

GUIDELINES FOR A HOSPITAL OR NURSING HOME VISIT

1. If the door to the patient's room is closed, ask a nurse if it is all right to enter. Then knock and enter upon invitation to do so.

2. Be very careful to note "No Visiting" and "Isolation" signs hanging on the door.
3. Look to see if the light is on over the patient's door. If it is, do not enter at all until the nurse has taken care of the patient's needs.
4. Do not touch, lean, or sit on the patient's bed. Even slight movement can add to the pain.
5. Size up the situation at a glance as you enter the room.
6. Always let the patient take the lead in shaking hands.
7. Upon entering the room take a position, whether sitting or standing, in line with the patient's vision, so that the patient is not required to move around in the bed.
8. Beware of letting the visit become a medical conference. Don't make a habit of sharing your own hospital experience or that of another with the patient. (The patient is the teacher, you are the student.)
9. Help the patient to relax by being relaxed yourself.
10. Do not carry emotional "germs" from one room to another. Rest if you need to.
11. Do not reveal negative emotional reactions through your voice, countenance or manner.
12. Do not visit when you are sick.
13. Do not make the visit too long. End on a positive note.
14. Don't whisper or speak in low tones to a nurse, to a member of the family or to anyone else in the sick room or near it.
15. You should usually leave when the patient's meal is delivered. (Ask—the patient will let you know.)
16. When visiting, make it a practice to speak to every patient present. Roommates are people too!

THE "WHAT IF?" SITUATIONS

What if this or that happens? What should you do? Here are some difficulties that a minister of care may confront.

1. Many times in a hospital or in a nursing home *the patient is under severe anxiety and stress.* This may not be obvious. An experienced minister of care learns to read the signals carefully. If you

sense that the patient's spirit is low, allow him or her to express the full range of emotions. Permit a wide range of conversation if this seems to be helping.

2. Sometimes *the patient has visitors* when you arrive. Your visit can happen when others are present, but more often you may wish to say, "Well, I see you have some friends now, would it be OK if I stopped back later today or tomorrow afternoon?" With a terminally ill patient, some member of the family may always be there. Your visit is as much to that family member as it is to the person being cared for.

3. The *television* present in nearly every hospital room can be a problem. Television is a great distractor. Frequently the patient cannot turn it off because another patient in the room is watching. Otherwise, you may offer to come back when the present program is ended. The patient may then accept your offer or suggest that you stay now. If the latter happens, you can simply ask, "Would you like me to turn the TV off?"

4. The medical staff performs routine and exceptional services all during a normal day. Your visit may be *interrupted* by doctors, nurses, even volunteers from the hospital. If it seems appropriate, offer to wait in the hall.

The relationship that you develop with the patient—even though you make only two or three visits—is very precious and is important to the patient. You will be surprised how long your visits will be remembered.

SOME SPECIAL CONSIDERATIONS

Nursing Homes

Nursing homes require a special commitment. They often demand a longer term, more predictable type of visit. Sometimes the visits require more patience, and sometimes a certain kind of advocacy (you may be the one to keep the nurse and professional staff, and even the administration, in touch with this person's needs and treatment). Nursing homes require a special gift of preparation. Not everyone is good at this. If this is your particular talent, offer to be assigned to a nursing home and to one or more people in that home on a long-term basis.

Families

Each person in the patient's family has his or her own particular reaction to the disease or disability. Remember the great spectrum of attitudes you will find. At times, there is a need for a minister of care to visit the mother or father or some other members of the family. A cup of coffee in the hospital cafeteria or a chat while walking down the hallway can be good for all concerned. Research with families of cancer victims shows how the family suffers. These families may need your care also. Respond to the individuals within the family and not just to the family itself.

Stress

The ministry of care is not easy. It takes its toll on many of us even if we are well prepared for it. Your attitude is the most important part of this ministry: be confident of what you are supposed to do and of what you are not supposed to do, of what you can do and of what you cannot. A minister can become overinvolved and overextended.

You cannot take on all the tribulations of every family you visit. The following are suggestions for dealing with stress.

- *Be aware.* Stay alert for signs of tiredness and irritability in yourself. If you feel nervous and anxious, recognize it, name it, feel it. Emotions have a habit of being heard one way or another.
- *Know yourself.* Know your breaking points. If you know today is not a good one for you, that is OK. Only you know yourself. Work from your experience.
- *Trust your emotions.* If you feel angry, sad, happy, scared, or hurt, allow yourself to feel that way. You probably have a very good reason. Knowing how you feel is initially more important than getting rid of how you feel.
- *Consider your alternatives.* What are your choices? What can you do? Mentally challenge yourself so you know what you can and cannot attempt. Time alone, a walk around the block, time in a chapel—these may help
- *Do something.* Even if you don't do something dramatic, do something. It will give you the feeling of being more in charge, more in control.
- *Reflect.* How did things work out? Do a quick "before and after" checklist in your head. This will allow for a faster process next time and you will discover more about yourself.

Silences

Silences will sometimes happen because of reflection and sometimes because people don't know what to say. Silence can be very awkward for the minister of care. Sometimes you may feel you are "on" to make the conversation flow. You may feel pressure to make the visit a "good" one. Remember that silence probably indicates only that the person is resting or thinking. The patient needs this silence. One solution to the silence problem is this: When you have said something and there is silence, give the person a full 60 seconds before you say anything more. This will force you to allow the silence to happen. You will see that it is not a catastrophe.

Rejection

It is the right of patients to see only the people they want to see. It almost never happens—but one day a patient may reject you as a minister of care and not want you around. That needs to be allowed and not challenged. Rejection by a patient is almost never personal. It seldom has to do with who you are or with the kinds of skills you have used. Rejection says more about the person who is rejecting than it does about the person rejected. Act professionally.

Anger

Hostility is sometimes directed toward the minister of care. We have to find out what life is like for this person, what this anger means, and what to do in this situation. In some cases, the person is blowing off steam. In other cases, they are venting real hostility toward you. You will always be in a better position if you can allow the anger to pass you. If you "catch the anger" you risk being hurt or angry yourself, and that will not help the situation. Allow the person to speak directly to you. "Don't assume" is a key phrase that will be very useful in this most difficult part of the ministry.

Errors

All of us make mistakes. Many of our mistakes, glaring to us, will never be noticed by others. Even when they are noticed, they may not make a big difference in the visit or in what happens. Errors can always be repaired.

Your Family and Personal Life

CHAPTER 9

As a minister of care you will be dealing with the problems and difficulties that other people face. You should be conscious of the impact your ministry will have on your family life.

In ministry of care, you deal with the negatives of life: illness, death, discouragement, the sense of loss in aging. This takes its toll in your life at home, but it is not the only effect of your ministry. The important times that you will share with the sick and elderly will be times when you are away from your family. You will be distracted from the concerns of your family. You will have concerns and worries and joys that your family cannot fully share.

It is sometimes easier to love strangers than it is to love those who are closest to you. To love strangers does not require the same commitment, or the same knowledge, or even the same skills as loving those who are closest. It can be very discouraging to those who live with you that you sometimes find more fulfillment, and more success, in ministering to strangers than you do in caring for your family.

Domeena Renshaw, M.D., of Loyola University of Chicago, makes the following suggestions about relationships. Apply them to your family life.

- *Trust.* Trust is the most basic of human emotions, especially in establishing satisfying, long relationships. Trust means that I can count on you.
- *Touch.* Basic human desire is to be touched physically and emotionally by another person. This desire goes across cultures and ages.

- *Time.* Everyone has 168 hours per week. You use some of it for work, some of it for sleep, some of it to eat. Then you may find that time which can be used for ministry at home and away from home.
- *Talk.* Being social animals, people also have an interest in finding out about others, understanding them, telling them about themselves.

Trust, touch, time and talk are necessary to healthy families, healthy marriages, healthy relationships. It is easy to see how to implement trust, touch, time and talk in a ministry situation with someone who is ill, someone who is in a nursing home, a friend or neighbor. But how do you apply these to yourself and your family? How, on a daily basis, do you implement trust, touch, time and talk with children and spouse?

These considerations might include: Does your spouse know the extent of your trust? Are people in your family aware of your concerns and fears in visiting the sick?

Have you "come in touch" with those around you (an easily neglected skill, one which people often find missing when they first recognize troubles in a relationship)?

Do you spend enough time with your spouse and enough time with your children? Many in parish ministry make time to be available to those around them. Many believe that the quantity of time with family is not as important as the quality. But it is vital that you acknowledge how much quantity you do need, and how much quality needs to be within that quantity of time. If you are not careful, you may be fooled into thinking that the few moments that you are able to spend with everyone together will make up for the time that you are away. Spend "enough" time with each person.

How do ministers of care keep their lives from getting too complicated? Successful ministers of care juggle the stresses of their lives with the stresses of the people they visit. They have certain strategies, values and tips that can be useful:

- Dr. Richard Westley, author and professor at Loyola University of Chicago, suggests a kind of personal motto, "Do what love requires." Whenever you get stuck, ask yourself what a loving response would be if you were the receiver. You will always get a fast answer.
- Management expert Peter Drucker advises, "Do first things first, second things hardly ever." Agendas have a way of growing beyond limits. Always set priorities. It doesn't always get done

on the same day, but the important things get taken care of.
- Author Alan Lakein writes, "Plan your work and then work your plan." Work goes faster if you take the time to plan it in some detail. Then, if you get lost, you have a roadmap. It also helps eliminate what isn't necessary.
- Rev. George Kane recommends, "People before things." A cardinal rule, hard to follow but a real life-saver when you are caught in the confusion of what happens next.
- "Help the healing happen." A way to know best what to do for someone: you can help them, you can't change them. You can influence, you can't make. You can promote healing.

In addition to recognizing the effect of this ministry on your family, it is also important to recognize the effect of this ministry on yourself. There will also be times when you will find yourself confused, when you won't know quite how you feel, when your feelings will become like a riddle. It is at these times that it is most important for you as a minister of care to look within yourself and to understand what it is that you are feeling. During these times you need to turn to resources, to reach beyond yourself to other ministers of care, to your parish leader, and the parish staff that is supporting you. Ministry of care cannot happen alone. It is strongly recommended that ministers of care regularly (monthly) "process" what is happening to them in this ministry. When you are confused, when you are in awe, when you find a richness that you cannot completely understand—these are the moments that need your attention.

CHAPTER 10

EVALUATING YOUR MINISTRY

In evaluating your work, do so with a proper attitude and a special perspective. Helping people in need can feel very good. As the helper, you can exaggerate your influence. It is not enough to evaluate this ministry just on the good feelings you get from it.

On the other hand, ministers of care often visit people who don't get better. In situations of chronic illness and death, it is easy to evaluate yourself as ineffective, of no use. These extremes miss the point of ministry: service in a special context.

Professional ministers are careful and realistic when it is time to evaluate their effectiveness. They know from experience that ministry can't easily be quantified. Good evaluation begins with good preparation. Knowing where you are headed is invaluable. The key here is the *goal*.

Business men and women have used written goals for many years. They begin their work with a deliberate aim—the end point. Ministers of care can do the same thing. You need to carefully (and prayerfully) anticipate what you want to happen. You may want to be a helpful listener, a resource person, a prayerful partner, a family companion, a timely visitor. All of these personal roles can be translated into goals.

To know where you are going is essential and so is the recognition of who you are—the *gift*. It is important to recognize and to be precise about what you have to offer as a person to another person. Perhaps you are lively, interesting, spiritual, happy, calm, accepting, patient, or any of the deep and important qualities that make up a gifted person.

You have to know, then, who you are (gift) and where you are going (goal).

The third quality is the link between the gift and the goal—the *guiding line*. The guiding line consists of all the little daily activities. These constitute your direction and purpose: how you said hello, what you did or didn't do.

When you feel "scattered," it may be that you are not as focused as you could be and that your less important activities are not in line with your larger goal.

When you feel "funny," it may mean that you are trying to minister as a friend or as a teacher did, instead of recognizing your own particular gift.

Evaluating Your Impact

It is rare that you get either positive or negative overt feedback that you can use. It is essential, then, that you evaluate your impact on those to whom you minister. Some suggestions:

1. Work from written goals.
2. Work toward one particular personal goal each year.
3. Take time weekly—daily is better—to review those goals and make corrections and adjustments.
4. Using a technique from industry, compare your progress with the same time last year.
5. Network with other ministers of care—use them as idea resources, human mirrors, and encouragers.
6. Pray over your ministry.

CHAPTER 11

SPECIAL PROBLEMS

Although many of the skills in your ministry will be used on a regular basis, there will be certain extraordinary situations which require special skills. When you are confronted with a particular problem, come back and reread parts of this chapter. Listed here are special problems that ministers of care confront.

Terminal Illness

Some people know that cancer will almost certainly kill them within a certain number of weeks or months, or that their child will die without an organ donor, or that an older relative is going to die because a weakened heart can't take much more. You will encounter such people at different points in death's approach. Terminal illness, as all illness, brings unique reactions from people. Much has been written about the stages that happen in dying; certainly reading and knowing that information can be helpful.

Some caution is necessary. *Do not apply textbook situations to real people.* You may recognize certain "stages" in a dying person, but never attempt to fit the patient into your understanding. Rather, attempt to enter into the world of the patient and so understand what this time is like for him or her. This holds true for ministry with the dying person's family. Approach the situation as if you are a blank piece of paper to be written on. The family writes on you, tells you their story, their particular situation. What is it like for them? Your job is not to provide solutions but presence and prayer.

Sudden Death

Most of us have had the shock of hearing of the sudden death of someone we knew or loved. As a general rule, pastoral departments in hospitals in the United States say that a family needs at least 72 hours notice to begin to cope as they prepare for the death of a loved member of the family. Automobile accidents, sudden heart attacks, murders: these often do not provide that time. For these families, the shock of the death and the shock of having to make funeral arrangements can be overwhelming.

The one "advantage" to a prolonged death is that people have a chance to say what they need to say, to think what they need to think, to pray what they need to pray. Sudden deaths don't allow this and that has important implications for working with the families. Ministers of care should seek to understand the particular needs arising from a sudden death.

When I Am Prevented from Helping

Ministers of care frequently ask, "What happens if I am rejected, if they don't want me?" Persons rarely reject a minister of care for reasons that relate to the minister's personality. Rejection usually has to do with attitudes toward the church or with the pain the person has understood to be caused by the church. It almost always has to do with the person rejecting, and not with the person rejected; but the hostility, sadness or anger will still be directed toward you. At such times, try to hold your tongue, draw on your own reserves, allow yourself to be "written on." Then make contact with another minister of care, your sponsoring parish staff, or some person, perhaps even your spouse, who can review the situation with you and look at it from the advantage of a detached third party.

In such ways, a minister of care must learn to take care of himself or herself. If you are unable to do that, reactions from others can gain unwarranted importance in your mind and destabilize your ministry.

Disabilities

Frequently, ministers of care encounter a person who is disabled. Blindness, loss of a limb, paralysis, the inability to talk or hear, or the loss of control over bodily functions may confront you when you visit people. For the more obvious disabilities, it is sometimes best to ask questions. "How long have you been without the use of your legs?" "When did you first lose your sight?" "Can you hear me now?" "May I help you down the hall?" "Would you like me to call the nurse so that he or she can assist you?" Such questions recognize the disability. They may put both of you at ease.

Sometimes the person will give you an opening to ask. "Well, I just don't feel good since the operation. I'm having a hard time walking." "I'm not in here for the paralysis, I've had that for years." "I don't see you very well because they are working on my eye. I may not have my vision for very long." Such quick and fleeting comments, "recognition comments," are for you to notice. When people volunteer information, they often expect you to ask a follow-up question. When you don't, it can seem as if you didn't hear them.

Disabled people sometimes have a strong sense of "I want to do it by myself." Be especially sensitive to this. When you want to help someone, ask if it is OK to help. If they say no, let it go. They want to do it themselves, even though it takes longer and they may feel worse. Don't be too quick to run and get a chair. You simply need to relax and be gentler.

Someone in a Coma

Occasionally you may visit someone who is in a coma. Your work will have to do mostly with prayer. It may also be a way to visit with the family. If you have checked with the nurses' station ahead of time and you find out the patient is in a coma, it is still appropriate to visit the person, even though the family might not be there. Some guidelines are helpful:

- *No matter what other people do, no matter what the staff does, no matter what you initially feel about the patient, never say anything in front of a person in a coma that you would not say to a person who is fully aware.* One of the senses that a person may retain when in a coma is hearing. People have come out of a coma remembering things that people said. It is respectful and medically correct to *always speak to them as if they can hear you.*
- If you are talking to the person in a coma or the people around that person, be very clear about who you are, why you are there, and what you are doing. Help that person to "follow the action" by saying things aloud.
- With the families of those in a coma, your quiet and patient listening will be tested. Coma is pure torture for families. They can't

communicate with the person; they often don't know if the person will ever wake up.

One-Time Visits

Sometimes you will be called upon to visit a person just once. A person may be in the hospital for routine tests or you may get a call late and the person is to be discharged soon. These visits are no different than any other visit, except for your attitude. Those who strongly prefer ongoing contact with people, who like to be friends, may not be the ones to do one-time visits.

It may be helpful to say things like, "If I can be any help, this is my phone number. Please call." Or, "This is the phone number of the rectory; have them get in touch with me." Do not say something like, "I'll be seeing you," because many times people take that literally. They think that you are promising to see them again, and that is just not the case.

Long-term Visits

Many ministers of care prefer these visits because they can develop a rapport with the person. They know what to expect and they can develop a friendship. Some, however, are not able to commit the time or the energy or perhaps don't want to have this kind of extended time with other people.

Be sure that you continue to have *pastoral* visits, and don't let them become simply social visits. That's a fine line, especially hard when you develop a friendship. Do a lot of reflecting on the visits, alone and sometimes with your minister of care supervisor. Taking care of yourself as a minister of care and as a person is a primary responsibility.

Sporadic Visits

You may see a person once, then a few months later a couple of times, and then perhaps not again for a year. These intermittent, unpredictable visits create a relationship, but also a frustration. Try to link the visits together, to be remembered from the last time. "How have you been? What's been going on since we met a few months ago?" Help the person reflect on the changes that have happened.

Sometimes these visits occur with cancer patients who go in for periodic treatments. Such people see you when they are involved with this special kind of pain in their lives. It is all right if you don't remember details about the person and have to ask again, but ask *in the context of knowing that you were there before.* For example, "You know, I've forgotten your children's names. Could you tell me again?" Such a question shows a continuity—and also shows that you are human. If you forget quickly, you will find it helpful to make notes after a visit and to keep a simple file to which you can refer if you visit weeks later.

Surgery and ICU (Intensive Care Units)

The minister of care is usually involved with the family rather than the patient during and immediately after surgery. Visiting hours for the ICU are often limited and are often "family only."

You are needed with the family. Probably you don't have to say very much. It is a time of waiting. Don't feel self-conscious. You are needed. Your presence is noticed and will be appreciated. Assume a calm composure, be available. Try to resist the temptation to "scurry" about from one person to another, getting coffee, making light conversation. This is a hard time for any family member—and for the minister of care.

Suicide and Survivors

The shock that accompanies this kind of death is long lasting. The care required for the family needs to be long lasting also. Some reading may help you understand this form of family tragedy, but you need not be an expert. Remember, this is still a death, a family that grieves, and a loss that needs your presence.

Alcoholism and Drug Abuse

These are two rampant diseases in our culture. When visiting someone who has been hospitalized, be sensitive to your role—a parish representative who physically communicates the support of the local faith community.

Psychological Problems

Occasionally you may be called upon to visit a patient in a psychiatric ward. Prepare your attitude carefully. Dismiss any of your notions about insanity and mental wards. Instead, remember that this person is hurting emotionally in a similar way to the patient who is hurting physically. After your preparation—treat it as a normal visit. Be aware of special visiting hours and consult with the nurses in charge before any visits. If necessary, you may have to call the doctor for permission to visit. This will take extra time, but it is well worth it.

Birth of a Baby

This can be a fun visit, but not always. Don't bring your expectations to this visit. Instead, find out what it is like for the new mother and father. This is *not* a time to speak of your children, your delivery, your advice on parenting. It *is* a time for prayer, parish greetings, and good wishes. Keep your antennae alert for concerns, cares and confusion.

Birth of a Sick Baby

Fear is an overriding feeling during these visits. Let the parents talk, cry, or be silent as they wish. Visit more than once and in rapid succession so they can learn to trust in your presence. Visit the baby, too. Pray.

Visiting Medical Professionals Who Are Ill

Don't be intimidated by this kind of visit. These people are afraid too. Sometimes they are at a real disadvantage because they know too much! Treat them as you would anyone else.

Caring for the Clergy and Religious

Again, no need for special treatment. Avoid "This should be you" or "I'm doing your job" jokes or comments. Often we overlook the very real human needs that these people have. Use your training—you are the minister for them.

CHAPTER 12

CONCLUSION

A minister of care must be a person who cares. The person who cares is one who has it straight that being present to another is what really matters, especially in times of pain, loss and stress. To share life's struggles with another, to articulate the prayer that emanates from the groaning of the Spirit within, to celebrate the dying and rising of the Lord in the concrete realities of people's lives—all this makes a difference.

Becoming a caring person is a lifelong process. In some ways, you are always beginning. You are always growing and deepening your perceptions and sensitivities.

A minister of care needs a hunger for life, a thirst for healing. This hunger and thirst somehow rises from a relationship with the Lord that is always becoming more conscious, more active and more alive. To foster this process of growth, attend to the following needs:

- Deepen your own spirituality, your way of looking at life and coping with life's struggles and challenges in the pattern of Jesus.
- Care for yourself. Listen to yourself in times of stress, in active moments as well as calm moments.
- Obtain formation and reflection on a regular basis: monthly reflection sessions with a competent supervisor of ministers of care, reading, sharing experiences of ministry and faith, programs designed for ministers of care, etc.
- Be affirmed as a minister of care. An official mandate from the bishop of the diocese says, "I am good enough to do this and the church recognizes this."
- Be accountable: know you count.

- Recognize some common pitfalls:
    cheering up a patient rather than being present
    offering sympathy rather than empathy
    passive listening rather than active listening
    not hearing what is meant

You are the people of God. God loves you and chooses you to make concrete the reality of the Lord's love for all humankind. Go forth knowing you do not go alone. Go with Jesus Christ!

APPENDIX

A STRUCTURE FOR THE MINISTRY OF CARE

How can a parish initiate, organize, train and provide for development of a local ministry of care? The key is a person who has the qualities essential to any ministry and something else: an ability to do the necessary research, to create effective structures which support the ministry, to provide resources to enrich the ministers, and to supervise the ministers regularly.

Research is the foundation for any successful outcome. The best initial research is talking to persons who are already involved in this ministry in other parishes. Also, tap into a network of coordinators of this ministry. Consult with the appropriate diocesan office. Check literature and media. Identify existing structures in the parish which support the ministry and find out how mutual support and cooperation can take place.

Setting goals is the next step. In beginning this ministry, it is important to keep the goals simple, measurable and achievable. For example:

> The goal of our ministry of care is to provide a presence, prayer and sacrament to parishioners who are hospitalized, residents of local nursing homes, and the homebound.

Once the goals are set, the planning process moves to designing strategies for implementation of the goals. Questions to be addressed include:

> How can the parish be educated to this ministry?
> Who will become ministers of care?
> How will they be recruited and selected?
> How/when will they be trained?

How will they be mandated/commissioned?
How will we know if we are achieving our goals?
How will we evaluate the formation process?
Once we have begun, how will we provide for newcomers to this ministry?
How often will we gather to share and process our experience of this ministry?
How will we continue to grow as ministers?

Education of parish members not only alerts them to this ministry, but also helps create an openness to accepting lay ministers of care. It sets the stage for calling forth those members who are gifted with compassion and care. This education should take several forms: articles in the Sunday bulletin, announcements at Sunday Mass, dialogue within already existing parish groups, parish staff commitment to support this ministry, one-to-one visits with potential ministers.

Selection of personnel is crucial. Having called for ministers, the coordinator interviews each person who responds. They discuss expectations, clarify roles and commitment, share vision and personal stories. Basic questions addressed during the interview include:

What is your personal experience of sickness/death/elderly/shut-ins?
Why are you interested in becoming a minister of care?
What are your expectations?
What gifts do you bring to this ministry?
To what area of this ministry do you feel called?
   hospital
   nursing home
   homebound
What is your availability for this ministry?

Before the interview concludes, it should be clear to both whether or not the person is accepted into this ministry. There should be a clear commitment from the potential minister of care to the entire training program, to a specified amount of time to be spent in this ministry, and to participation in the monthly reflection session with other ministers of care.

When all potential ministers have been interviewed and identified, it is wise to call them together for an orientation session. At this session the candidates meet one another (and experienced ministers of care, if the group already exists). The orientation should then provide information on the theology of ministry, allow candidates to share their stories of responding to this ministry, allow them to hear experiences of those who have been doing this work, and offer a chance to ask questions. Before concluding, all pray together.

The training program for the candidates may be that provided by the diocese, the deanery, another parish, or the local parish. One model of an approved training program includes six two-hour sessions with the following content:

Experience and Theology of Illness
Basic Skills of Visitation
Ministry to the Aging
Death and Dying: Implications for the Minister
Theology of Eucharist and Communion to the Sick
Prayer and Pastoral Visitation

When the training program is concluded, the ministers of care are publicly commissioned at a Sunday celebration of eucharist. Mandates are presented to the ministers; these indicate that the minister is called by the bishop to care for the sick and homebound. A bulletin announcement of this commissioning, listing the names of the new ministers, is a further step in the education of the parish and an affirmation of this ministry.

The monthly reflection session provides a forum for ministers to share their experience, process their feelings (which is especially important when ministering to terminally ill persons), and continue their development as ministers. These sessions aid in the ongoing supervision and evaluation of the ministry and are essential for the growth of all involved.

SAMPLE MEETING FORMATS

A.
1. Gathering in a warm, friendly, welcoming space

2. Sharing led by coordinator or designated person
    Questions to evoke sharing:
    What are you learning?
    What do you need to learn?
    What has been your experience of ministry in the past month?
    What questions do you have about your ministry?

3. Break

4. Input from the coordinator on specific area previously requested by ministers

    5. Closing prayer led by group member
B.
    1. Gathering
    2. Introduction of speaker for evening
    3. Input on specific topic by speaker
    4. Break
    5. Group process/interaction on topic
    6. Group response reported to speaker
    7. Speaker response and wrap-up
    8. Closing prayer
C.
    1. Gathering
    2. Sharing of experience of ministry
    3. Break
    4. Continued sharing of experience of ministry
    5. Closing prayer

Content for additional formation during reflection sessions can focus on ministry to the bereaved, ministry to children, spirituality of the minister, theology of sacrament, anointing of the sick, developing communication skills, role playing (visits to the sick, for example) and other concerns expressed by group members.

Annually each person should be invited to evaluate his/her experience and commitment as a minister of care. Opportunity for individuals to meet with the coordinator should be provided. After reflection and evaluation, the minister then renews commitment for another year or chooses to bring closure to this involvement.

Caring for the ministers of care is a special responsibility of the coordinator. Caring for the coordinator is just as important. This includes support structures which enable the coordinator to grow in responsibility for others, to invite others into this ministry, to develop skills of leadership, to establish good order and integrity in this ministry. Such support structures are found in networking with other coordinators on a diocesan or deanery level. If no such network exists in a local area, start one! Call other coordinators together to share experiences, ideas and prayer. Do this regularly and it becomes a network of support.